NGIYA YINTANGA JAPARRIKA

PUFFIN BOOKS

UK | USA | Canada | Ireland | Australia
India | New Zealand | South Africa | China

Penguin Random House Australia is part of the Penguin Random House group of companies whose addresses can be found at global.penguinrandomhouse.com.

First published by Penguin Random House Australia Pty Ltd, 2019
This edition published by Penguin Random House Australia Pty Ltd, 2020

Text and illustrations by Tiwi College Alalinguwi Jarrakarlinga,
with David Lawrence & Shelley Ware

Tiwi College Students
Rusinya Brooks, Michaeline Moreen, Michaeline Mungatopi,
Bella Puruntatameri, Freda Puruntatameri, Jessica Puruntatameri,
Kim Stassi, Lindy Timaepatua, Jean Tipiloura, Demi Warrior

Printed and bound in Australia by Griffin Press, part of Ovato, an accredited ISO AS/NZS 14001 Environmental Management Systems printer

A catalogue record for this book is available from the National Library of Australia

ISBN: 978 1 76 104136 5
penguin.com.au

Penguin Random House Australia uses papers that are natural and recyclable products, made from wood grown in sustainable forests. The logging and manufacture processes are expected to conform to the environmental regulations of the country of origin.

NGIYA YINTANGA JAPARRIKA

Written and illustrated by

TIWI COLLEGE
ALALINGUWI JARRAKARLINGA

With David Lawrence & Shelley Ware

PUFFIN BOOKS

TIWI ISLANDS

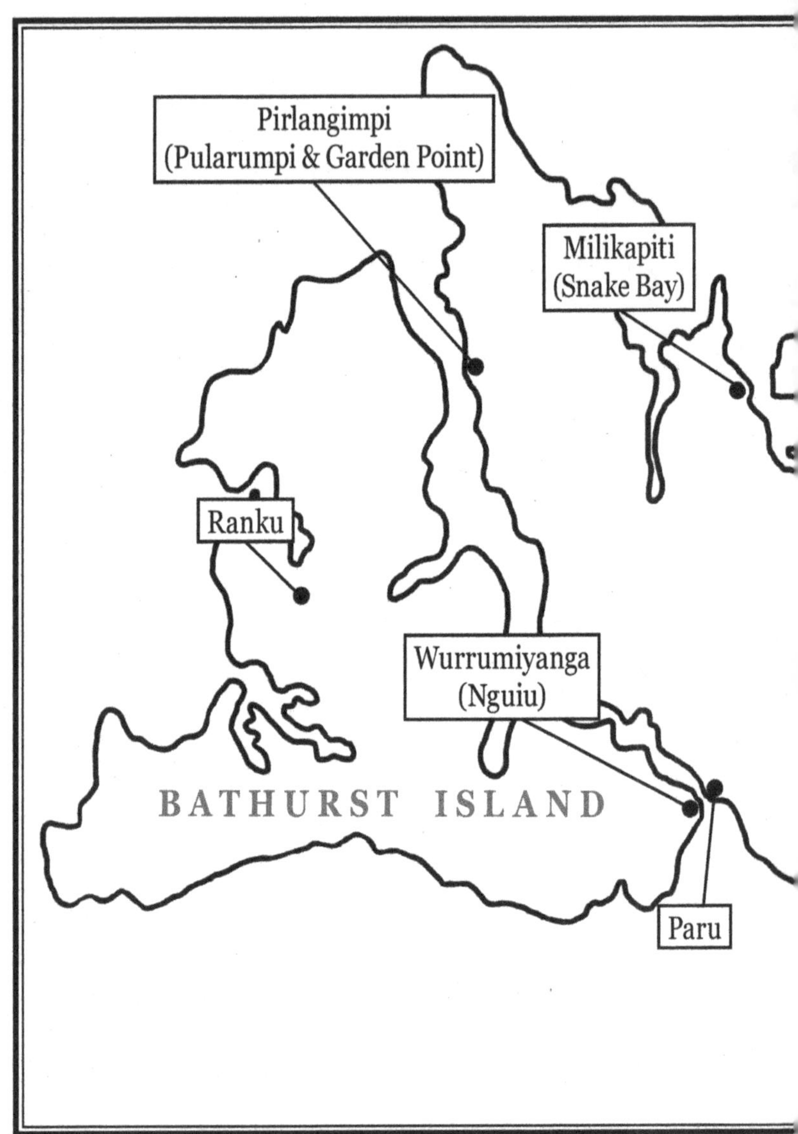

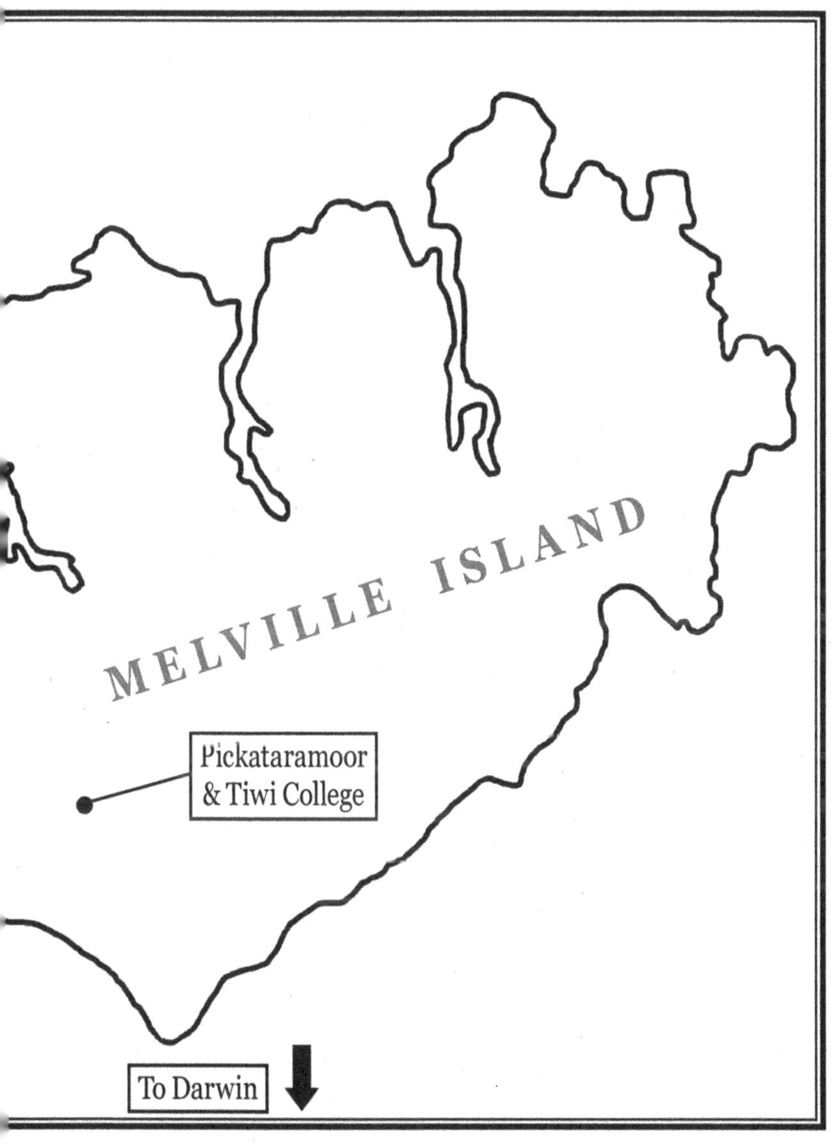
MELVILLE ISLAND
Pickataramoor
& Tiwi College
To Darwin

AUSTRALIA

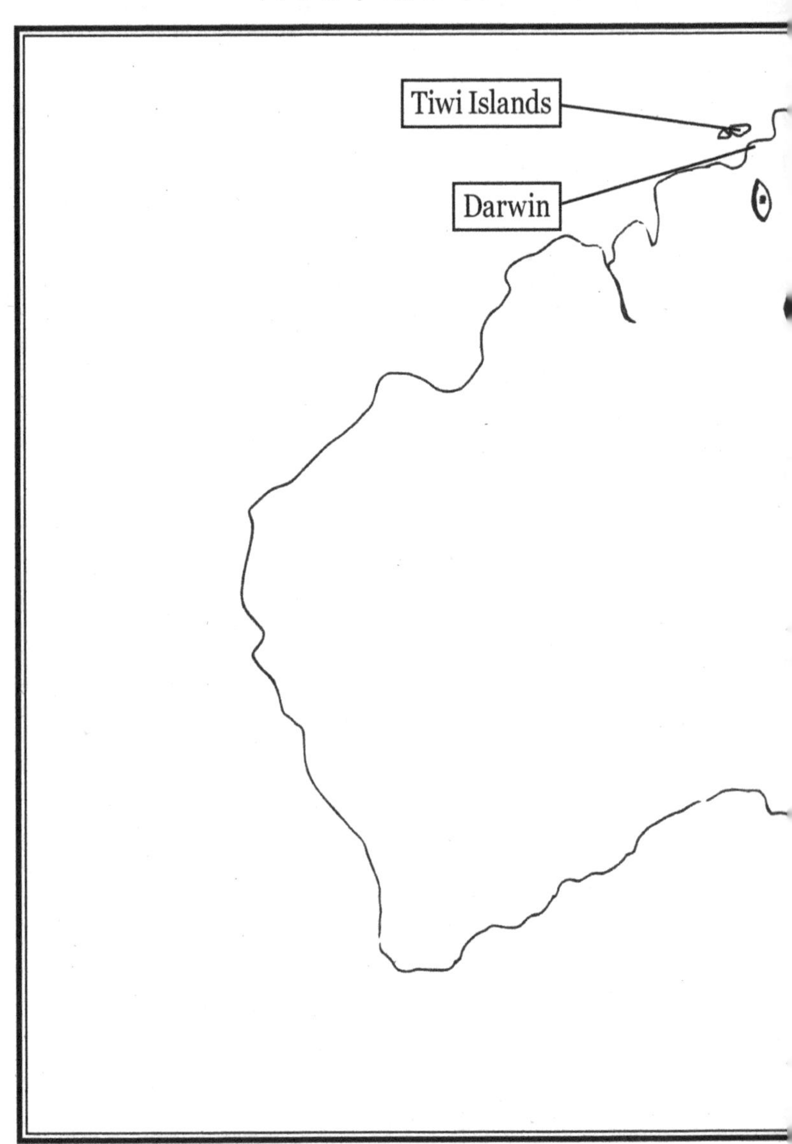

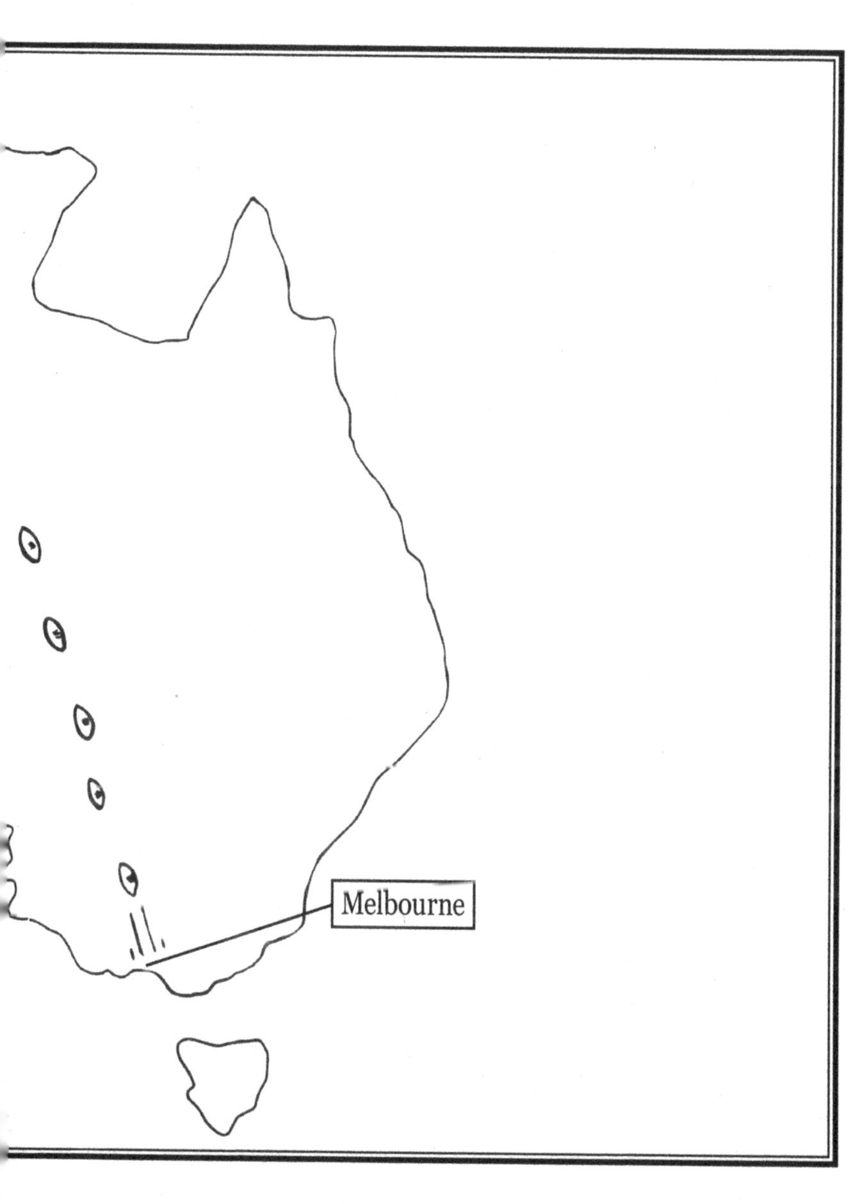
Melbourne

Japarrika is the Tiwi name for the Greater and Lesser Frigatebirds, which the Tiwi people call a storm bird. It lives on the shore or in the mangroves and when locals see it in the sky it tells them there's a storm coming.

'Japarrika' is also the name of the team song for the home side, the Tiwi Bombers, in the NT Football League.

Ngiya Yintanga Japarrika
means 'My Name is *Japarrika*'
(the Storm Bird).
In the story this name was given
to Kay-Bell by her brother, David,
and *Japarrika* has been a good
luck symbol for her.

Kay-Bell woke up from her sleep and remembered it was her last day at home. Today she was going to say goodbye to her family and her two best friends. As Kay-Bell sat on her bed, she thought about how she was going to miss everyone.

After she got everything organised, David and his family

dropped Kay-Bell off at the airport in Pickataramoor. She got her bags out of the car and headed straight to the check-in.

Before she entered the plane, her family, Aunty B, Dema, Jess and her beautiful teacher, Tictac, waved goodbye.

'*Nimpangi*,' they said.

Kay-Bell hopped in the plane and she silently cried all the way to Darwin.

When she arrived in Darwin, she had to catch the taxi to the main terminal at Darwin airport. She boarded a Qantas flight and headed to Melbourne. In the middle of the flight, she had a flashback of playing footy in the Lightning Series Competition. She remembered her brother calling her the name '*Japarrika*' – the Storm Bird. It made her think about how she had played like a super star and how her dream to play AFLW was unfolding. The support and help from her big brother and her friends had helped her to get to where she was now.

As Kay-Bell was sitting in her seat, she wondered what it was going to be like being away from home, living a different lifestyle and eating different food.

She was really excited to play for the Essendon Bombers VFL. Kay-Bell realised that this was an opportunity for her to represent her culture, family and where she comes from.

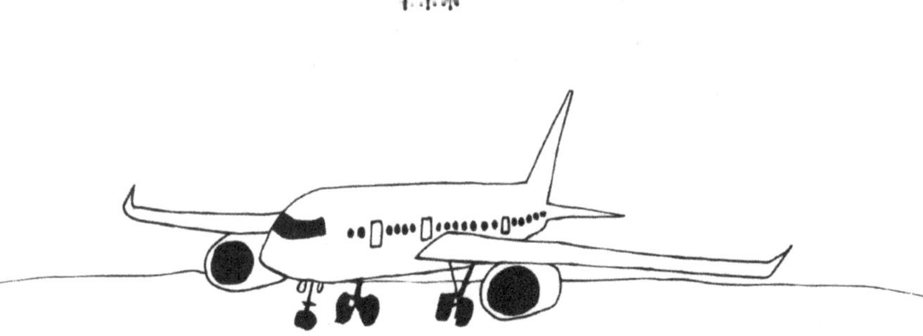

After four long hours of flying from Darwin to Melbourne Kay-Bell was outside the arrivals terminal. The first thing Kay-Bell noticed was the weather. It was different to where she lived, like the air-conditioning was on. It was windy and cold; Melbourne seemed to be a bit cloudy. And there was lots of traffic, noises everywhere coming from different directions and people rushing past her.

She chucked her jumper and trousers on and then headed straight to catch the taxi to the apartment where all her teammates lived.

When she arrived at the apartment, the coaches were there to welcome her.

'Hi Kay-Bell. I'm Ashley. I'm your coach,' said Ashley. 'This is Taj, the assistant coach.'

'*Awana*. Sorry, I mean hello,' said Kay-Bell.

Then the coaches took Kay-Bell to her room where she would stay. When she opened the door, she saw her enemy, Sam, sitting on her bed and looking at her as she entered the bedroom.

Kay-Bell gasped. *Oooh no, what is SAM doing here!* she screamed in her head.

Kay-Bell realised that Sam had made it into the VFLW team for Essendon too, and now she had to live with her and another girl named Molly.

Kay-Bell thought sharing the house with Sam was going to be bad. It turned out to be even worse than she could ever imagine!

On the first night Kay-Bell wanted to have a shower, but Sam was already in the bathroom. Kay-Bell waited and waited and waited . . . for almost one hour.

When she finally went into the shower she turned on the tap and screamed, 'Arrrhhhhh – Sam, you used all the hot water.'

'I don't care!' Sam yelled back.

When Kay-Bell tried to go to sleep that night, Sam was playing loud music in her bedroom. Kay-Bell yelled, 'Can you please turn down the music because I'm trying to go to sleep?'

Sam called out, 'I don't care!'

The next morning Kay-Bell woke up and walked into the kitchen to have breakfast. The kitchen bench was covered in dirty dishes. Sam's dirty dishes!

'Sam, come in the kitchen and clean your dirty dishes now,' Kay-Bell said.

'I don't care,' said Sam.

Molly said, 'Don't worry, Kay-Bell. I will give you a hand.'

Kay-Bell was mad at Sam but she was excited to head down to training that afternoon.

Essendon's training ground was called the Hangar and it was nothing like Kay-Bell had ever seen before. Firstly it was huge! It had a giant indoor training room, changing rooms and a weight room. Outside it had two big ovals – one was the size of the MCG and the other was like Docklands stadium.

'Ahhh! Deadly,' said Kay-Bell and Molly at the same time.

The Essendon coach, Ash, yelled out to all the girls, 'Oi, come inside for a meeting.'

They sprinted inside and stood in front of the coach. Ash was short and had long, straight, black hair. Her arms were folded and she had a frown on her face.

WOW! She made Aunty B look friendly, thought Kay-Bell.

'All right, everyone. I expect you to start eating healthy food, training really hard and doing everything I tell you to.'

All of a sudden the assistant coach Taj said, 'Hey, why did the footballer cross the road? Cos Ash told her too!'

Everyone burst out laughing as Ash glared at Taj.

'That's why you're the assistant coach,' said Ash.

The players went out on the oval where Ash gave them instructions for some complicated training drills.

I am so confused!, thought Kay-Bell.

So she turned to Sam and asked, 'Do I run to the left or to the right to get a handball?'

'The right,' whispered Sam.

So Kay-Bell ran to the right.

'The left, Kay-Bell!' screamed Ash. 'I told you to run to the left!'

Kay-Bell felt embarrassed and it was even worse when she heard Sam laughing.

***

That night back at the unit Kay-Bell was fuming!

But Molly helped calm her down by talking to her in Kriol about hunting. They both loved hunting and Kay-Bell loved that Sam couldn't understand them.

'You better not be talking about me,' said Sam.

Kay-Bell looked at Molly and smiled.

At least I have one friend down here, she thought.

3

The Windy Hill change rooms had never been so quiet. The players were nervously putting on their boots and pulling on their jumpers. Suddenly Coach Ash yelled out, 'This is it, girls! This is what we have been training hard for all pre-season. Your first game playing as an Essendon Bomber.'

So everyone started to scream

and get excited for the game. Taj called them in as a group and cracked a joke to make them laugh. Then he yelled, 'Let's get out there and win this game!'

Kay-Bell was nervous and happy to be running out for her first game for the VFLW Bombers. She looked at Molly, who seemed just as nervous. 'Molly, let's just go out there and have fun.'

Molly smiled and said, 'Yeah, Sis.'

Kay-Bell was used to being the star of the game but she quickly realised it was a very different game than what she was used to playing back in Tiwi. The girls were bigger and stronger. They tackled harder and they hurt more when they hit. The structure of the game was difficult for her to learn and it was even harder for her to play too. The game was faster than she was used to playing as well.

Kay-Bell started to worry and panic. She started to drop the ball and she made a lot of mistakes. Kay-Bell forgot some of her teammates' names. Molly and Sam looked like they knew what they were doing, which made Kay-Bell make even more mistakes.

Kay-Bell yelled out in Tiwi, 'Bringem *ngarra*. Bringem *ngarra*.'

The other players didn't know what she was saying and it distracted them. Eventually they stopped passing the ball to her and Kay-Bell was left out of the game. She felt sad again and thought she wasn't going to be an AFLW star after all. She just didn't have what it took.

Unfortunately the VFLW Bombers lost their first game of the season. After the game in the rooms, Ash told Kay-Bell she would start on the bench next week. She wanted Kay-Bell to watch the game plan in action and learn from her teammates and how to play as part of the team.

Kay-Bell thought, *Nothing could possibly get any worse*.

After she got changed she grabbed her phone and saw she had a missed call from David.

She called him back. She knew straightaway from David's voice something wasn't right.

Kay-Bell asked him, '*Kama?*'

David replied, 'Aunty B is *jana* and she needs to go to Melbourne for some tests.'

Kay-Bell was upset and started to cry. She was very worried about her Aunty B.

'Don't worry. She'll be *pumpuka* soon,' said David.

David tried hard to calm Kay-Bell down and told her not to worry too much. They said their goodbyes and hung up the phone. After speaking to David, Kay-Bell wanted to go home back to Tiwi.

4

She couldn't help but feel sad and worried about Aunty B. Even though Aunty B was mean, rude and even horrible at times Kay-Bell was still concerned. It didn't help that David's voice had sounded so upset on the phone. Aunty B had arrived in Melbourne for her tests and Kay-Bell couldn't wait to visit her at the hospital after training.

Throughout the training session Kay-Bell was making mistakes left and right. She was so distracted and caught up in her head and thoughts that she didn't hear her teammates call her name. When she did she was surprised by the sudden booming of voices. Kay-Bell turned around to see what was happening and came face to leather with a football. The force was too much and knocked her off her feet. There was a lot of laughter from her teammates but Sam was cackling the loudest.

'Stop laughing,' said Mouse, the team captain.

She outstretched her hand and Kay-Bell grabbed it. Mouse pulled Kay-Bell up to her feet.

'Thanks, Captain,' Kay-Bell said.

'No worries. It's the end of training and you can go home now if you want,' said Mouse.

Kay-Bell was embarrassed and wanted to leave as soon as possible.

She took off running, with her training gear stuffed in her bag, and headed for the hospital.

By the time she reached

it Kay-Bell was still feeling embarrassed and was sweating from training. She was relieved to reach the air con in the hospital. She asked a nurse where Aunty B's room was. The nurse showed Kay-Bell to the ward where Aunty B should have been. Kay-Bell walked around until she heard a loud but familiar demand: 'I don't want this soup. I want my magpie goose curry!'

'Aha, found her,' laughed Kay-Bell.

As Kay-Bell walked to the curtains a nurse rushed past her to get out of the room and away from the old lady. Kay-Bell pulled the curtain slightly just to get a glimpse of a familiar-coloured beanie. Red and black – Bombers colours.

'*Aga*, Aunty B, that's you or what?'

Aunty B was startled by the sound of Kay-Bell's voice. 'Ah, thank goodness you are here. These mob don't even know how to look after me.'

Kay-Bell was relieved to see her aunty looked all right and not as bad as she had imagined when David was on the phone to her. 'So what's wrong, Aunty? Heard you were *jana*,' asked Kay-Bell.

'Yeah, I feel a bit sick. I don't even know what's wrong with me. All I know is I'm feeling sick,' said Aunty B. She continued, 'Look here, Kay-Bell. I am sorry for how I have treated you. I really am sorry. I should treat you more like a niece than a slave. After losing my sister I was scared to lose you. I felt like I had to have more control over your life and that way I could keep you safe, just like I told your mother not to go out driving that time because of the bad rain and she didn't listen. Hard headed, just like you.'

Kay-Bell was lost for words. She noticed something odd happening under Aunty B's beanie.

It looked like . . . nah couldn't be.

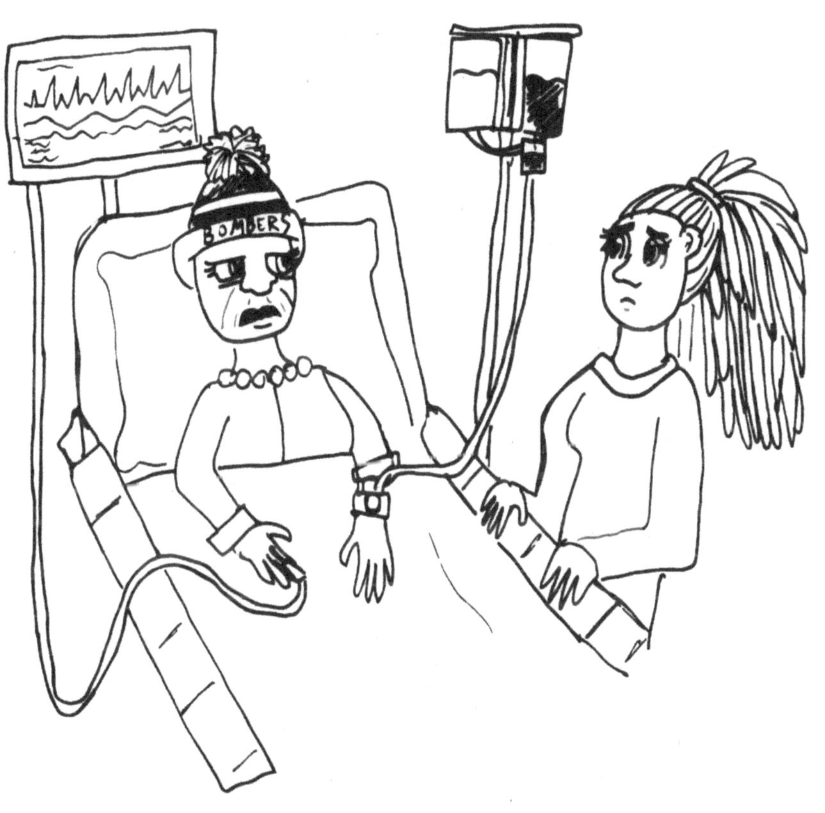

5

Aunty B returned home to Tiwi after her tests in Melbourne. She looked like she was going to be okay. Kay-Bell felt really homesick after seeing Aunty B leave and she wanted to go home too.

Later that week, Kay-Bell and her teammates were training at Windy Hill. It was raining, it was cold and it was windy. All Kay-Bell was thinking about was the hot, warm weather back at home. As Kay-Bell ran to mark the ball in the forward pocket, she slipped on the sideline. Sam saw what happened and started to laugh and make fun of her.

Then Kay-Bell got up and said to herself, '*Awi*, I'm giving up now 'cause I'm not good enough.'

Molly could see that Kay-Bell wasn't happy. She ran over and said, 'Hey, you right, owat, Kay-Bell?'

'Nah, I give up,' replied Kay-Bell.

‘Aye, what for? You too good to give up,’ said Molly.

That night Kay-Bell was in her room, crying to go back home.

A few minutes later Molly came running into Kay-Bell’s room and told her that someone had come to see her. Kay-Bell wiped her tears and went to see who was at the door. She opened it and saw Tictac standing there.

Kay-Bell jumped with excitement and said, 'When you came, Tictac?'

'I came today. I got biggest mob *yinkiti* for you,' replied Tictac.

'*Awi*, for real? Don't lie, because I don't like this *yinkiti* we eat here in Melbourne.'

Kay-Bell called Molly to come so she could introduce her to Tictac. 'This is my teacher,' she told Molly.

'Hi, where you from?' asked Tictac.

'I come from Katherine,' said Molly.

Then they walked to the kitchen. 'You mob want some magpie goose curry stew?' asked Tictac.

'Sure, we would love to.'

The bush tucker made Kay-Bell feel like she was back at home.

Molly adored her first taste of magpie goose curry stew, Tiwi style. They both enjoyed the curry goose so much, they went back for seconds.

***

The following week was the Indigenous Round. Kay-Bell was

in the changing rooms, getting ready for the war cry. Suddenly her best friends, Dema and Jess, came in to surprise her. Dema snuck up on Kay-Bell and tapped her on the shoulder and said, 'Surprise!'

'What you mob doing here?' said Kay-Bell.

'*Awi*, we came to see you play and we got free tickets because we designed this year's Indigenous jumper you are about to wear.'

'Oh deadly, I'll wear it with pride.'

Then Kay-Bell and her teammates walked out to the field. They all had paint on their faces and stood together, proud of who they were.

Kay-Bell had butterflies in her tummy because she had been on and off the bench all season. Tictac had spoken to her before the game and reminded her that *Japarrika* was part of her. Just seeing Tictac, Jess and Dema in the crowd helped her feel confident and supported. She knew it was her time to shine. Kay-Bell was ready to run amok ... and she did. She played the best game she had ever played in her life.

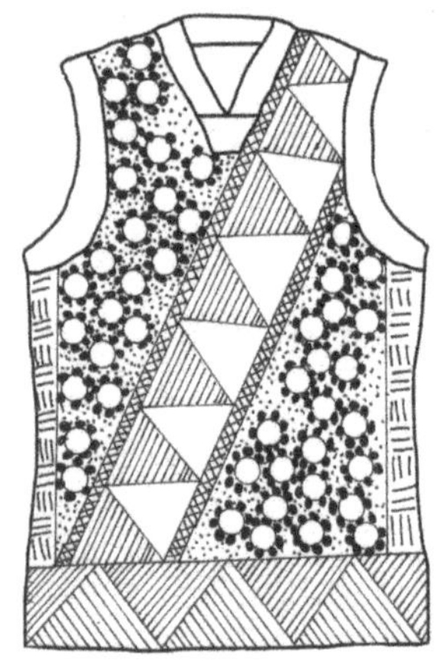

6

Kay-Bell and Molly were getting used to living with each other. They laughed a lot and became good friends.

It's like living with a cousin, thought Kay-Bell.

At Essendon, Ash and Taj both were really happy with how all the players were communicating with each other.

This had a lot to do with Captain Mouse who was really happy to be leading the team. She would make sure the girls in the team got along and that no one was left out. She always made sure all the girls were ready for the game – pumped, wide awake, drinking plenty of water and doing all different stretches before they headed out onto the ground.

***

On the next game day, there were just a couple of minutes

left before the first bounce.

The coaches announced to the girls what position they were playing in first quarter.

Kay-Bell then asked Molly, 'Hey Molly, what position you playing?'

'I'm playing in the mid-field. What about you?'

'I'm starting at centre half forward,' replied Kay-Bell.

The crowd cheered as both teams ran straight out onto the field.

The siren went and it was game on!

Captain Mouse took a big jump for the ball. She grabbed it,

stepped around her opponent, then bounced the ball. Another player tried to tackle her, but she stepped around her and the crowd went wild. As she was running towards centre half back, she saw another opponent who was heaps bigger than her.

Captain Mouse suddenly looked confused as she wasn't sure what to do. Luckily she noticed Sam running past her.

Phew! She now had one of her teammates shepherding her.

Bang! Sam smashed into the opponent, knocking her to the ground. The crowd cheered again as

Sam leapt to her feet after her big hit.

Mouse noticed in the distance Kay-Bell was making position towards the boundary line.

But Kay-Bell's opponent was right on her. Kay-Bell had to get rid of her. So at the last second she did a beautiful U-turn, which confused her opponent. She ran towards a different position to get that mark and shouted, 'Bringem *ngarra*. Bringem *ngarra*!'

Bang! What a beautiful kick from Captain Mouse. Suddenly, the opponent that Kay-Bell had lost sight of, came rushing towards her.

Kay-Bell thought to herself, *Mmm, I should do a specky!*

Up went her left knee onto her opponent's shoulders, then the right knee. Kay-Bell put all her weight down on her opponent and took the beautiful mark. The crowd went crazy as Kay-Bell took a couple of steps back and took a deep breath.

She faced the four white poles then ran in to kick the ball. What a beautiful banana kick! It just flew like a rocket through the middle of the two big white sticks. Kay-Bell felt fantastic. It was the best goal she'd ever kicked.

But then she heard a voice from the crowd; it was an old man. And he yelled out something terrible. Something racist.

Kay-Bell was devastated. And she didn't get another kick from then on.

7

After the game Kay-Bell felt like she needed to talk to her big brother about what had happened at the game. Tears rolled down her cheeks as she dialled his number.

'Hey David here, please leave a message and I'll get back to you.'

OMG SERIOUSLY! thought Kay-Bell. There must be another

big storm back at home so that's why there is no reception.

Kay-Bell left the game without telling anyone. When Molly realised that her friend had gone she started to feel so worried. Molly told Captain Mouse what had happened.

***

Molly and Captain Mouse went to chat to Kay-Bell that afternoon.

Captain Mouse said, 'Hey Kay-Bell. I'm sorry you had to hear that racism. The club is going to put a big statement on social media saying how wrong it is and we are not going to put up with it.'

Hearing this news, Kay-Bell felt better. She had seriously been thinking about giving up on footy.

The reaction to the club's statement was amazing!

It went viral so people read it all over the world and it even made the front page of a newspaper. Kay-Bell got heaps of messages of support. Her favourite was a photo of her two friends Dema and Jess holding up a Tiwi flag and an Aboriginal flag.

A few days later Kay-Bell's family flew down to Melbourne for the weekend just to show their support for her too. At the next game Aunty B, her big brother David and her nieces and nephews – Lomani, Henry, Anaiah and little Ana – were there.

Kay-Bell couldn't believe she had a family who cared so much to support her. But she also couldn't believe that there were complete strangers showing their support too. There was a sea of Aboriginal flags and people cheering her on at the game.

Kay-Bell felt proud of who

she was and just as proud to be a strong Tiwi girl living away from home and representing the Islands. She was proud of her culture and history.

With all the support Kay-Bell began to believe in herself again. 'I am *Japarrika*, the Storm Bird. I have everyone behind me,' she said.

And for the rest of the season, she played some deadly footy.

8

Kay-Bell couldn't believe they had made it to the VFLW Grand Final. Her whole body was shaking as she tried to warm up with the team.

'I have to do this for Aunty B,' she said, sprinting onto the field. Her heart was beating so fast, she thought it was going to burst out of her chest.

From the first bounce Molly scooped up the ball and booted it to Kay-Bell, who kicked it to Sam for the first goal of the game.

During half-time in the change rooms, Kay-Bell was exhausted and dripping in sweat. She sat next to Sam and Molly, who looked just as exhausted.

'Come on, girls. Let's do this!' yelled Ash. 'You need to stick on your players.'

Third quarter flew by – it was goal for goal. The crowd was going crazy!

Molly yelled out to Kay-Bell, '*AGA*, MAKE SURE YOUR

EYES ARE ON THE BALL.'

Kay-Bell replied, 'YO, YOU MAKE SURE PUNCHEM THAT BALL, PROPER LONG WAY.'

In the final moments of the game, Molly booted the ball to Sam. Out of the corner of her eye, Sam spotted Kay-Bell sprinting to the wing. Kay-Bell bumped her player and was open. Sam kicked to Kay-Bell, who marked it on her chest just as the siren went. Kay-Bell knew they were four points down and had to kick a goal.

She took a deep breath, pulled up her socks, lined up and kicked it straight through the goals.

'Aaaaaaargh!' roared the crowd.

Sam and Molly ran to Kay-Bell and they all hugged. Kay-Bell couldn't believe it, they had won the VFLW Grand Final. The players celebrated together and when they presented the medals, they added the icing on the cake by announcing Kay-Bell had also won Goal of the Year.

***

A few days later Kay-Bell and Molly headed for Tiwi. Molly was excited to see Kay-Bell's home.

As they got off the ferry, old Jeff yelled out and pointed to Molly. '*AGA*, YOU, COME HERE.'

Molly got a fright. She thought she was in trouble.

‘I know you,’ said Jeff. ‘I’m your uncle.’

Kay-Bell looked at Molly and said, ‘I’ll call you *cujin*, cos I call him uncle too.’

Kay-Bell took Molly hunting in the mangroves for her first time. Molly thought it kind of smelt funny but she didn’t mind. Kay-Bell showed her how to find *jukwarringa* and *piranga* in the slimy, smelly, slippery mud. They even got two *kirrimpika*.

After hunting Kay-Bell said to Molly, ‘*Aga*, we go look for *yilinga*.’

‘What’s *yilinga*?’ asked Molly.

‘It’s carpet snake,’ replied

Kay-Bell. She explained that they had to search for a hollow log. A few minutes later, they found what they were looking for. Kay-Bell pulled out a mirror. Using the sun's reflection on the mirror, she lit up the inside of the log.

‘Woohoo,’ said Kay-Bell ‘We’re having *yilinga* for dinner.’

They chucked everything in the troopy and headed back home. Kay-Bell was happy and since she had just got her licence, David let her drive home too.

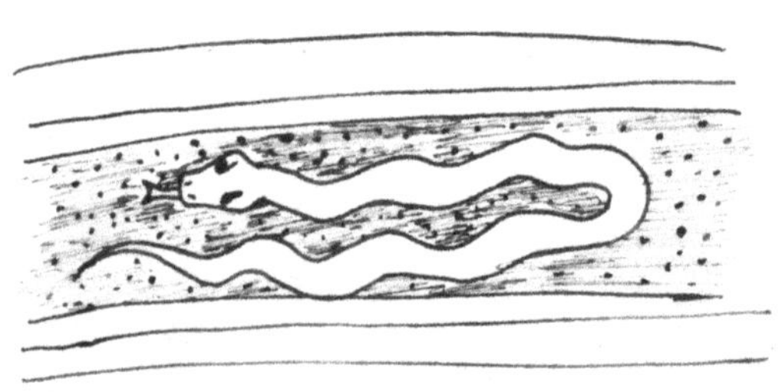

Back at the outstation Aunty B was getting the fire ready. As they got out of the troopy, Aunty B said, ‘*Marri*, what you mob bin get?’

‘We got biggest feed, Aunty B,’ said Molly.

As the sun went down, they sat around the fire and waited for their dinner to cook. The delicious smell of the bush tucker made their bellies rumble.

‘It’s so good to be back home,’ said Kay-Bell.

9

Kay-Bell and Aunty B were sitting under a mango tree, eating some sweet and juicy mango. Kay-Bell got a phone call from the AFLW. They told her that she needed to go back down to Melbourne for the draft.

'Nah, I can't go because my aunty is sick,' said Kay-Bell. 'I need to stay and look after her.'

They explained to Kay-Bell she could watch it on TV instead because it was going to be on live stream.

Kay-Bell rang her big brother and told him about the draft pick tomorrow.

The next day David and his little family went to Aunty B's house to find Kay-Bell and Aunty B sitting in the lounge room, waiting to watch the draft.

'*Marri*, is it on, owat?' said David.

'Nah, nothing yet, Bro,' said Kay-Bell. 'We're still waiting.'

Kay-Bell was very nervous. She

was biting her nails and her legs were shaking.

'Kay-Bell, you right owat, *Bumbis*?' said Aunty B.

'*Kuwa*, I'm right, Aunty B. Just nervous,' she said.

Kay-Bell was so happy to be at home with her family, watching the draft but she wished her mum and dad were there to see her fulfil her dream.

Kay-Bell got a text from Sam:

Hey sis good luck on the draft.

The draft started and everyone was nervous and happy for Kay-Bell.

'You ready, *abigo*? Draft pick

number one is my deadly sis,' said David, grabbing her with one arm.

'Ahh relax, Bro, too early,' said Kay-Bell. 'I just hope I get picked.'

'*Awi*, be quiet. It's starting,' shushed Kylie, David's wife.

Everyone was staring at the screen as the announcers introduced the opening of the draft pick.

'We will start the draft with pick number one. Going to the Adelaide Crows, from the Northern Territory, Tiwi Islands. Kay-Bell.'

The whole family jumped with joy.

Kay-Bell tapped Aunty B. 'Ahh Aunty, did they say my name, owat?'

'*Kuwa*, they bin say your name. Are you deaf, owat, *Bumbis*?' laughed Aunty B.

David started dancing around. 'Kay-Bell! My *abigo*, you made it,' he yelled.

Kay-Bell still couldn't believe it but they showed her highlight package on the TV. 'It's really happening.'

A few picks later came Sam's name. She too had been picked to Adelaide Crows.

'Of course,' laughed Kay-Bell.

She was happy that she would at least know someone in Adelaide.

Kay-Bell's phone started blowing up with lots of text messages. The one that caught her eye was from Molly.

Congrats cujin. Hopefully next year for me. Come visit me in Melbourne sometime.

10

Kay-Bell was sitting in the Adelaide Crows' change rooms surrounded by her new teammates. She was waiting for the jumper presentation. She kept looking around as her family had said they would be there.

Ting. Kay-Bell's phone chimed with a notification. She opened the post and saw that Sam, her once enemy, had posted a photo of the three girls – Kay-Bell, Sam and Molly – from their season in VFLW and was wishing Kay-Bell luck with her first game at the Adelaide Crows. Kay-Bell looked up from her phone to Sam sitting on the bench across from her. They smiled at each other. After everything they had been through it was nice for Kay-Bell to have a familiar face on her team.

The coach started to speak. Kay-Bell still hadn't laid eyes on David and the kids. 'We are about to get started with the jumper presentations. Many family members have made special trips to be here today for this important moment in your AFLW careers,' she said. The coach continued, 'I will start calling out the numbers.'

'*Awi, maka* this mob? They should be here,' huffed Kay-Bell. 'They are always leaving everything until last minute.'

The coach rattled off a few numbers and players and then got to Kay-Bell's. 'Introducing number 17, new player all the way from the sunny Tiwi Islands . . . Kay-Bell.'

Kay-Bell looked around quickly. She still couldn't see David and

the family. As she walked towards the coach Kay-Bell focused properly. She then noticed it was Aunty B who was holding out the jumper for her. She took the jumper in one hand and wrapped her arms around her aunty.

Aunty B started to cry with happiness and whispered, 'Your parents would be so proud and I am also proud of you, *Bumbis*.'

Aunty B was wearing an Adelaide Crows shirt and beanie with pride. Kay-Bell then noticed David and the kids standing closely behind her. Everyone had made it. She felt proud to have her family there supporting her, especially because her mother and father couldn't be there.

The coach finished calling out

the rest of the players and told the families that they needed to leave because the girls had to do their warm up and come back for a team chat. As the players ran out for their warm up, Kay-Bell felt someone tap her on the arm.

It was Sam. 'Can you believe we are about to run out onto this field for the first time as AFLW players?'

'No, I can't believe it. Hey, Sis, this is mad,' responded Kay-Bell.

The team did a few warm ups led by the new captain before the coach called them back to the rooms to hear the game plan.

Kay-Bell started to get nervous. She bit at her nails and could barely concentrate on what the coach was saying.

The captain placed her hand on Kay-Bell's back to give her some encouragement. 'You'll be right, Kay-Bell – number 1 draft pick. Live your dream and smash it!'

The team grouped up and ran together through the opening onto the field. Kay-Bell could hear her whole family cheering from the stands.

'That's my sister!' yelled David.

'Go, Aunty!' screamed the nieces and nephews.

But the loudest of them all was Aunty B. 'That's my baby *Japarrika*.'

Kay-Bell waved to them. At that moment Lomani accidentally knocked Aunty B's Adelaide Crows hat off.

Kay-Bell couldn't believe her eyes. 'Woooah, what the? *Ang*, that *murrula* bin grow back!'

The hat had been hiding Aunty B's new white afro.

Kay-Bell couldn't stop laughing and smiling as she ran through her team banner. She thought to herself, *I can't believe my dream is coming true. All my hard work and I am finally on the big stage.*

Running to her position at full forward the sun hit her eyes. Kay-Bell looked up. It couldn't be. There was a cloud shaped like *Japarrika*. Behind she could see the sun streaming down and she even felt the sun hitting her shoulders. Kay-Bell knew in that moment her whole family had made it to the game – her mum and dad were watching down on her too.

GLOSSARY

abigo – little sister

aga – hey, used when talking to a female

awana – hello

awi – hey

aya – hey, used when talking to a male

bumbis – niece

cujin – cousin (Kriol)

jana – sick

Japarrika – storm bird

jukwarringa – mud mussel

kama – what

kirrimpika – crab

Kriol – the most widely spoken Aboriginal language used by an estimated 20,000 Aboriginal people in communities across northern Australia.

kuwa – yes

maka – where

marri – hey what

murrula – hair

ngarra – here

ngiya – me

nimpangi – goodbye

piranga – long bum

pumpuka – good

yilinga – carpet snake

yinkiti – food

yintanga – name

SLANG GLOSSARY

ang – ah (used when something good happens)

aye – hey

bringem – bring them

deadly – awesome

mob – people, large amount

owat – or what

proper-really or proper long way – a really long way

troopy – a troop carrier, a large four wheel drive that carries up to 10 passengers

AUTHORS AND ILLUSTRATORS FROM TIWI COLLEGE

Students

Rusinya Brooks

Michaeline Moreen

Michaeline Mungatopi

Bella Puruntatameri

Freda Puruntatameri

Jessica Puruntatameri

Kim Stassi

Lindy Timaepatua

Jean Tipiloura

Demi Warrior

Teachers

Ashlee Healey

Dianne Moore (Tictac)

with David Lawrence & Shelley Ware

ABOUT DAVID

David Lawrence is a comedy writer/performer who accidentally became a children's author in 2008. He has written for numerous TV shows including *Hamish & Andy*, *Comedy Inc.*, and *Talkin' About Your Generation*. His books, *Anna Flowers,* the Fox Swift series and the Ball Stars series have sporting themes and use humour to tackle issues such as bullying and racism in schools. David still hopes to play AFL football and win a Brownlow Medal ... but at age 50-something, it's going to be tough.

His newest book series is Maxi the Lifeguard.

ABOUT SHELLEY

Shelley Ware is a proud Yankunytjatjara and Wirangu woman from Adelaide, South Australia, who currently lives in Melbourne. She is the host of AFL.com's show *Colour of Your Jumper*.

For the past decade or so, Shelley has worked in the media as a radio and television presenter on both local and national AFL football news shows. She has become one of the most respected and recognised female presenters of AFL football in the country.

Shelley also works part-time as a teacher at Parade College in Melbourne where she is currently the Indigenous Education Officer.

INDIGENOUS LITERACY FOUNDATION

Our vision is equity of opportunity. As a national book industry charity we aim to reduce the disadvantage experienced by children in remote Indigenous communities across Australia, by lifting literacy levels and instilling a lifelong love of reading. We do this through our three core programs: Book Supply, Book Buzz and Community Literacy Projects.

This book was produced as part of the ILF Create Initiative. This program partners young Indigenous women at Tiwi College with publishers and mentors to create (produce stories), cultivate (build knowledge) and motivate (grow self-esteem).

Find out more at ilf.org.au

CREATE INITIATIVE

Ngiya Yintanga Japarrika was produced as part of the ILF Create Initiative. In October 2019, ten young Indigenous women from Tiwi College visited Sydney where, together with Penguin Random House staff and two mentors – David Lawrence and Shelley Ware – they created this book.

We thank everyone who helped to make this project happen.